CAN'T TAKE ME ANYWHERE

CAN'T TAKE ME ANYWHERE

NEIL FULWOOD

All rights reserved. No part of this work covered by the copyright herein may be reproduced or used in any means—graphic, electronic, or mechanical, including copying, recording, taping, or information storage and retrieval systems—without written permission of the publisher.

Printed by imprintdigital
Upton Pyne, Exeter
www.digital.imprint.co.uk

Typesetting and cover design by narrator
www.narrator.me.uk
info@narrator.me.uk
033 022 300 39

Published by Shoestring Press
19 Devonshire Avenue, Beeston, Nottingham, NG9 1BS
(0115) 925 1827
www.shoestringpress.co.uk

First published 2019
© Copyright: Neil Fulwood
© Cover photograph by Neil Fulwood

The moral right of the author has been asserted.

ISBN 978-1-912524-34-1

ACKNOWLEDGEMENTS

Some of these poems, or earlier versions of them, originally appeared in:

The Black Sheep Journal, Central Coast Poetry, Clear Poetry, Dead Snakes, Dissident Voice, DIY Poets, The Fat Damsel, Ink Sweat & Tears, The Lake, London Grip, Medusa's Kitchen, Message in a Bottle, Ol' Chanty, Outburst, Peeking Cat Poetry, Picaroon Poetry, Prole, Rasputin, Riggwelter, Section 8, The Stare's Nest and *VerseWrights*.

'The Zero Hours Tarot' was anthologised in *We Shall Overcome: The Anthology* (Goya Independent Press, 2017).

'Mambo' was anthologised in *Strike Up the Band*, edited by Merryn Williams (Plas Gwyn Books, 2017).

'A Bigger Chair' owes a debt to 'Table' by Edip Cansever.

Ana Braojos-Molina's contribution to 'The Prince of Torremolinos' is gratefully acknowledged, as is Laura James's to 'Never Buy New Shoes for a Corpse' and Mandy Harrison's to 'The World According to Dads'.

My thanks to: Viv Apple, Alan Baker, Liz Baugh, Lucy Beckett, Daniel Brenchi-Sluman, Amy Clarke, David Cooke, Andy Croft, Paula Fulwood, Harry Gallagher, Kate Garrett-Nield, Robert Kenchington, Kathy Kieth, Joanne Limburg, John Lucas, Roy Marshall, P.A. Morbid, Harry Paterson, Grant Tabard; and to family, friends and comrades.

For Richie Ellis Claydon

CONTENTS

1. Platform Zero — 1

Can't Take Me Anywhere	3
Whistle Softly and Walk Slowly Away	4
Trending	5
Toucans at Their Rest	6
Never Buy New Shoes for a Corpse	7
Platform Zero	8
What They Bleep Out on *Ice Road Truckers*	9
Dockyard Crane	10
The Joy of Trucks	11
Work	12
Monkey Awakes	13
20 Zone	14
Karajan in the Rush Hour	15
No Money Down	16
Directions	19
Services	20
Coast Road	23

2. The Ambridge Fountainhead — 25

England	27
The Ambridge Fountainhead	28
The Prince of Torremolinos	30
The Zero Hours Tarot	32
Lizard	34
Peril	35
Light Cavalry Overture	37
A Snake in the Grass	38
Sleepless Beauty	40
Alice	43
Man Friday at Peace	45

3. FOXTROT AT THE GOLF HOTEL   47

Still Waters   49
Cork   50
We Renew Our Vows in the Presence of the Auto-Wed Machine   51
A Bigger Chair   52
All Day Long   53
Mambo   54
The World According to Dads   56
Siri Attempts a Polite Response   57
Foxtrot at the Golf Hotel   58
The Lighthouse in the Stars   59

1. Platform Zero

CAN'T TAKE ME ANYWHERE

It's me making the too-loud comment
for the benefit of a lager drinker

in a real ale pub. It's me asking for brown sauce
in the Michelin-starred restaurant.

It's me prompting that roll of the eyes, that
shake of the head. It's me photobombing the Mona Lisa,

Whistler's mother, the barmaid at the Folies-Bergère.
It makes you despair of me even more

that I know what year Manet painted it. How to spell
Folies-Bergère. Where the accent goes

WHISTLE SOFTLY AND WALK SLOWLY AWAY

The paint tin on its side, sumping
a matte white map of Iceland
over the hallway carpet. A pan
dislodged from the hob, Bolognese
making a murder scene of the kitchen.

Bone china, in the family for decades.

Signed first edition with coffee stain.

Football and greenhouse. Just
whistle, whistle softly, and walk away.

Whistle softly and walk slowly away.

TRENDING

I would like to take your hashtag
and use it as a cheese grater
until I've flaked away everything
that's trending. I would like to
reshape your hashtag, make a TV aerial of it

and see if I can find an arts documentary.
I would like to snap off one upright
from your hashtag and use it
to air-conduct Wagner. Then snap off
the others to leave a square

and use it as a frame for a photograph,
in black and white, of someone
staring across a landscape where fields
and horizon have their own idea of distance.
The kind of place where there's no signal.

TOUCANS AT THEIR REST

Toucans in their nests agree
Guinness is good for you
Try one today and see
What one or toucan do
          – 1940s Guinness advert

Their feathers are shabby, their bills
chipped like the veneer on a badly-used table
that fetches nothing at auction.
Their eyes are dim. Some joker
keeps moving the horizon further back.

They flew in squadrons once, pints
of the stuff beak-balanced.
The opposite of bombers, not
a fluid ounce of their cargo spilled.
Or they occupied weathervanes

and watched men carrying girders.
And on every corner a pub
with a Popeye-bicep'd landlord
and a choice of bitter, mild or stout.
A pub today would confound them.

Their cages are comfortable enough;
besides, the sky doesn't hold
the same appeal. Endlessness daunts
when endurance is finite.
They watch TV instead. They haven't

recognised an advert in decades.

NEVER BUY NEW SHOES FOR A CORPSE

Never leave anything in a Wetherspoons
that isn't nailed down. Never exceed
the maximum dosage, recommended
daily intake or the bandwidth of a warning.

Never look back in anger, forward in apathy
or side-to-side while shaving. Never look up
for fear of diarrhetic pigeons. Never buy *The Sun*.
Never take no for an answer except in this case.

Never bet on black, double down or stake it all
on the turn of a card. Never use Dostoyevsky
as a "how to" manual. Never cheat or lie. Admit
nothing. Never put all your bastards in one egg.

Never give your real name at *those* kind of venues.
Never give an assumed one at a signing session.
Never say never unless quoting this poem.
Never use social media at 3AM. Even when sober.

Never take a politician's word without a pinch of salt
roughly the size of Lot's wife. Never put an X
in the box without consulting a spotter's guide
to the lesser of two evils. Never let your guard down.

Never answer the door or the phone. Never answer
the call of the wild unless personally certificated
by Jack London. Never stare into the sun, howl
at the moon or misquote Walt Whitman while stargazing.

Never miss a beat, a chance or an episode of whatever.
Never shoot your TV when other viewers are present.
Never listen. Never leave contradictions unattended.
Never doubt, never believe, never strive, never give up.

PLATFORM ZERO

This is not Adlestrop. No birds singing
and whether the dull parallel of the rails
ends up in Oxfordshire or Gloucestershire
is anyone's guess. It's dark and I can't see

the end of the platform. It rained earlier.
The service was delayed shortly after
the view stopped being worth looking at.
Two hours between a sewage treatment plant

and a haulage yard and it wasn't as if
the trucks were those big gleaming rigs
you'd imagine hauling dangerous loads
across Alaska. Now I'm here, standing

on platform zero and it's either the railway
equivalent of Bruckner's *die Nullte* or
my second-class Twilight Zone ticket
has brought me to the start of a journey

I never took. Either way, the café's closed.

WHAT THEY BLEEP OUT ON *ICE ROAD TRUCKERS*

Loneliness. The thickness of ice.

The core of despair
slammed like an eight ball
around the pool table of macho talk.

The freezing point of diesel.

The twenty-two words for *snow*,
the two hundred for *cold*,
the two thousand for *fucking cold*.

DOCKYARD CRANE

See it from above—a helicopter shot
in a movie—and it's a piece of equipment
doing a job. The arc of the gib
steady, measured: cargo shifted to ship.

See it from the ground and it's as if
the iron man from the children's story
had done twenty years on the day shift,
survived the lay-offs, paid his union dues.

See it by night under a whittled-down moon,
nothing moving but the watchman's torch,
tomorrow's paper full of bad news—
it seems like a relic, a skeleton of rust.

THE JOY OF TRUCKS

The nub you latched the grease gun onto
and gave it a squeeze—the grease nipple.
As if anything about the subframe
of a heavy goods vehicle could be erotic,
as if giving anything a squeeze
might be a turn-on in this environment,
or being supine on a crawl-board
shade one's thoughts toward a masseuse
and a happy ending. Rather consider
the contortions required by the confines
of a sleeper cab and understand why
the breathless history of erotica
never offered up *Tropic of Scania*
or *Lady Chatterley's Trucker*, even
in a truncated edition where Mellors
spends five days on the road, one day
servicing and just wants a shower and a pint.

WORK
i.m. Derrick Buttress

Your poems put in their ten or twelve hours
a day at the factory or in the sweatshop—
they milled and soldered, cut and stitched

and emerged with callused syllables,
the knuckles of their lineation red raw.
They knew the value of a keen eye

and a process executed at speed.
They knew the cost of minimum wage
and the banter of the underprivileged.

Your poems saved the best of themselves
for the knocking-off whistle,
scrubbing up well for an evening

at the dance hall or picture palace,
on the *qui vive* for the girl who'd transmute
Ava Gardner's smoulder from the silver screen

to the streets of Broxtowe. Two cigarettes
lit from the same match, a pint
and a dry white wine from the last

handful of change, her name coyly omitted
from their stanzas as they made their way,
your poems, casually back home

barely thinking of work tomorrow.

MONKEY AWAKES

In the movies this would be the magical scene,
fairy dust floating in 3D, John Williams
coating the soundtrack with syrup.

The stuffed toy come to life! The child
who *believes*! The best falsehoods
a Hollywood budget can buy!

Here's the reality: a house without children,
two grumpy adults dragging themselves
to the anti-Dreamworks of the office

and Monkey, hearing the car unzip itself
from the driveway, renouncing
his floppy inertia, Monkey

yawning and stretching and wondering
why they don't just quit if it
pisses them off so much,

Monkey hoisting himself onto the sill
and shoving the window open,
toking on fresh air, Monkey

readying himself for the trek downstairs,
the battle with the percolator,
the state of the fridge.

20 ZONE

Dead skin sloughs off me, settles
around the gear lever. A layer
of dust coats the dashboard
in slow-motion. The Jones's cat
watches me pass but loses interest.

My hair concentrates on the business
of hippie-length growth. I sprout
a beard worthy of a Solzhenitsyn emoji.
The kids waiting at the bus stop
pass exams and have kids of their own.

There's a General Election. A handful
of celebrities die and a few others
are caught doing things they shouldn't.
Donna Tartt publishes a new novel.
A small galaxy winks out of existence.

I reach the end of the estate; indicate left.

KARAJAN IN THE RUSH HOUR

Symphony N° 1, final movement. This recording
from the maestro's second Brahms cycle,
the 1970s account where small planets are destroyed
and mere mortals fall to their knees,

half-deafened. I'm in traffic, late in getting to a job
I hate, and my imagination shifts gears
between highbrow and lowbrow. I see myself
as Magneto from the *X-Men*, only

divested of cape and helmet. A baton instead.
But the gestures are the same: imperious,
commanding, dismissive of the unimportant things.
A movement of the wrist, a small flick

of the baton and the car in front of me upends,
is tossed aside. The white van: cast back
into whatever automotive netherworld spawned it.
The *Apprentice*-fixated management type

in his red Porsche: an iron filing yanked toward
the magnet of its own conflagration.
The careful driver, he of 10mph less than the limit
and a six-car-length stopping distance:

a cube of scrap metal, no-claims bonus screwed.
Cyclists? Oh pray for them in their hour
of terror. Pray, indeed, for every bit of traffic
from here to where I don't want to be.

And when I get there, that endless crescendo.

NO MONEY DOWN

The angel has flown the bony perch
of my right shoulder,
the demon departed the left.

Nil-nil in the age-old struggle for the soul
of an unimportant man?
No such luck. They've relocated,

that's all—the angel
to a commune where off-grid
and sustainability are the gospel *du jour*;

the demon to a car dealership.

The angel's wings waft soft approval
when I recycle or cycle
or use public transport. The demon

has easy credit terms and a muscle car
sleek under showroom lights,
a V8 nightmare,

chassis cast in sulphur
on the Hades production line,
tank brimming with Devil-piss;

a car straight out of every drag race,
every road movie, every
rock 'n' roll song:

whitewall tyres, chrome grille,
two-tone paint job—
whorehouse red and midnight black;

a car to race through the back streets in,
a car to cruise the boulevards in,
a car to park on that crest of scrubland

overlooking the city,
break the seal on a fifth of bourbon,
toast the sunset that shrinks the avenues

to a wiring diagram of glass and neon,
and drink to the transience
of pretty people in favoured places,

envied and ogled for one night only;

a car to park by the chainlink fencing
at the end of the runway,
hood down and radio drowned

by the noise of a jet in its sluggish ascent,
silver girth of fuselage
carving the sun to a metal penumbra;

a car to stake against the turn of a card,
a car to drive 500 miles straight
to see a concert or meet a girl,

a car to slow down for a leathery hitchhiker
with a guitar case
and a twang in his voice

that's strangely familiar, whose stories
make darker that stretch of the night
where the mind wanders

and the white line fades, the car drifting,
its vanishing point somewhere
beyond the ghostly hulks

of a Porsche Spyder, a Buick Electra
and a Plymouth Savoy last seen abandoned
at the Golden Gate Bridge,

doors open, keys in the ignition.

DIRECTIONS

Take that passage from Dickens—the one
where fog seeps into the first page
of the novel—and substitute snow.
Take a road map and trace the few miles

from Jedburgh to the English border;
reflect that you're south of Edinburgh,
nowhere near the highlands, far from
the headiest of single malts. Take a landscape

that has lost definition, road and field
indistinguishable from sky. Snowflakes
muffle the windscreen wipers.
Rear wheels fishtail. Your right foot

hesitates; leaves the accelerator alone.
Take heart in the approaching shape,
a piss-yellow smudge that resolves
as snowplough. Take account of the driver,

padded like a test dummy in pudgy layers
of winter wear—this in April—and take
as gospel his admonition to turn round,
turn round while you can, and head back.

SERVICES

after 'Barton in the Beans' by Joanne Limburg

Through tiredness, flagging fuel gauge,
full bladder or the irritable ache

of legs too long employed
at the business of clutch/brake/accelerator,

pull into one of them - circle their acres
of concrete for a parking space,

avail yourself of their grim conveniences,
their bad coffee and chain outlets.

Route and destination immaterial,
they sing the smashmouth poetry

of their own names: Annandale Water,
suggesting a calm surface and sailboats

in silhouette, a pen pal in falsehood
with Ferrybridge, where the expectation

is deep-sixed twice over. They're not
the only motorway double-act: Knutsford's

all thuggish, daring you to spill its sludgy coffee,
an unwelcome break cellmate

to Strensham, chewing on its ugly syllables
and wanting to know if you've got a problem.

It's safer to say you haven't, like it's safer
to say Burtonwood sounds like a colliery

not a firm of conveyancers. Like it's safer
to keep your mouth shut about Gordano

gorging on a *Sopranos* box-set binge,
or Killington Lake angling for a role

in a stalk 'n' slash horror movie franchise, or
the J38 Truckstop mistaking its locale

for some cherry pie slice of Americana
halfway between Chuck Berry

and The Doors. Elsewhere, the touchstone's
pure Englishness: Cullompten coughing

then spelling its name, South Mimms
like something out of P.G. Wodehouse,

tea in bone china, the daintiest of cakes;
Pease Pottage providing material

for the lewd-at-heart and graffiti artists;
Toddington traipsing to centre stage

like a tubby comedian whose jaded japing
is always at the other bloke's expense.

Newport Pagnell puffs out its cheeks,
a practice run of petulant syllables,

while Castlebellingham point blank refuses
the courtesy of a space bar's punctuation.

Clacket Lane could have been a previous abode
of one Albert Steptoe Esq. Tibshelf's

amenities are supplied flat-packed,
an Allen key and an hour's patience required.

Woolley Edge is a fuzzy and far-flung piss-break
on the very edge of forever. Circle

the acres of parking-space concrete,
stretch your legs, baulk at the prices.

COAST ROAD

Back-handed gusts of wind come off the water,
side-slam the car. I'm thinking of that poem by Heaney:
the heart caught off guard. I'll trade that
for sharpened driving skills, on-point response
to the switchbacks and gradients of a road
supplemented with escape lanes—last-ditch
slow-downs for the brake-failed, the wheel-locked.

Earlier, the shoreline was a photo-opportunity:
a silver medal for the play of light on water;
crofters' cottages, open land; the railway line
daring itself closer to the edge than the road.
Now: snow. Great driving flakes of it
from a grey-white sky. Push on? Turn back?
I'm thinking there's no real difference.

2. The Ambridge Fountainhead

ENGLAND

Scratch the surface and fingernails snag
on Facebook posts arm-banded with hate.

Spade the earth with boot heel encouragement
and feel the bite-back of roots twisting whitely.

Christen the dull metal of the plough, drag
trenches through topsoil; repeat

till the land is scarred. Dig deeper. Sink holes.
Send Euclids rumbling into the depths of open cast.

Let shit-brown mud coat the yellow buckets
of JCBs. Unearth bones and broken skulls.

THE AMBRIDGE FOUNTAINHEAD

for Lee Tombs

Howard Roark stands naked in the upper window
of a guest house twee enough to resemble
a tea cosy with fenestration. And laughs.

Twilight comes on—that thin, apologetic colour,
English breakfast tea without milk—
and Howard Roark pushes the blacker slab

of his barrel-chested shadow out across the village.
The shadow of an über-mensch. And he laughs.
Laughs that it has come to this. The absurdity of it!

The absurdity of England, of Ambridge, of being
asked to build a barn! Laughter answers him back:
a sharp jab of a laugh from the direction of The Bull—

a laugh like the lid slamming down on a tuneless piano.
And he knows what they're saying. Well, let them talk,
let them laugh. He'll build their barn, god damn it,

a barn that surpasses purpose, function and history;
a barn in glass and concrete; a monolith
of phallic supremacy that will tower over St Stephen's

and render the word of God detumescent in the face
of the works of Man. Oh yes, he'll build their barn.
He'll redefine the concept of barns to allow for the word

"heroic". A barn where tractors will clank and heave
like armoured vehicles. A barn to which fields of corn
will bow, self-reaped. A barn wherein a man

who's man enough will clash in his naked manliness
with the volcanic lust of a woman unattainable to lesser men,
perhaps that aristocratic one from Lower Loxley Hall,

and their copulations will be like dynamite
in a slate quarry. Howard Roark pictures his über-barn
and the awestruck fear of peasants on the day

of its investiture, and he laughs, laughs, laughs
for half an episode until his landlady stomps upstairs
telling him to keep the noise down and put his trousers on.

THE PRINCE OF TORREMOLINOS

> *I suppose the Bulstrodes will go and live abroad somewhere ... That is what is generally done when there is anything disgraceful in a family.*
>   — GEORGE ELIOT: Middlemarch

Money has put him where he is now,
a man of business in a tourist trap.
Money took him through Fuengirola
and Benalmádena, an expatriate
carving a niche. Greased palms,
slick talk, bodies oiled and bronzing
lined up along the beaches like hot dogs
waiting to be turned on the grill,
pockets waiting to be turned out
in the bars. A loan here, a favour there,
a signature on the dotted line.
His name assumes a currency.
    Bulstrode.
    Bull. John Bull.

Deals done cash in hand, off the books
and auditless. Some local muscle
to back him up, a reputation
ambivalent enough to make a tough guy
hesitate, but not scare investors off.
Money accruing. Money rubbing up
against itself, non-consecutively.
Money dancing its graceless tango.
A couple of bars, a casino, interests
in a hotel complex. Money brought him
here, made him what he is now—
the prince of Torremolinos.
    Bulstrode.
    Bull. British bulldog.

Twisted as a pound sign, in thrall
to the value of the Euro, he curses
the nubile acres of the beach
should his day-old copy of the *Daily Mail*
cost him more than it did last week.
He turns his back on the tanned ranks
of girls languorously arranged
as if auditioning for reality TV,
turns his back on the lads strutting
their pimply delusions. They're nothing
till evening fetches them in, nothing
till their lusts and their wallets are his.
        Bulstrode.
        Bull. Businessman.

THE ZERO HOURS TAROT

for Daniel Brenchi-Sluman

You have drawn ten cards. They are arranged
in the Celtic Cross. The first card is the Present;
it is crossed with the Challenge. These are
the Hangover and the Ten Hour Shift respectively.
They are cards of the Major Arcana.

The third card is the Past; it indicates how you came
to be in this position. It is the Knight of Pints,
a card of the Minor Arcana, and depicts a barman
happy in his work. No purveyor of short measures, he.

The fourth card is the Future. Whether the immediate
or mid-term future, I cannot say. Be aware
it is not the final outcome, merely another stage
in your journey. It is the Ten of Wage Slaves;
its illustration will be familiar to you.

Cards five and six symbolise Above and Below,
the former aspirational, the latter a slap in the face
from your subconscious. You have drawn cards
of the Major Arcana: the Double Rollover Lottery Win
and, below, the card of Existential Dread, easily
recognisable by its mirrored surface
and your ashen yet perspirant reflection.

Card seven is Advice. The querent is encouraged
to reflect upon this card and heed its lesson.
You have drawn the One of Benefit Claims,
a pitiful card that has little business in this position.
Reversed, it is often blocked by the Major Arcana.

The eighth card is the card of External Influences,
depicting those forces over which the querent
has no control. This is the most tumultuous card

of the Major Arcana, its illustration still divisive:
hugs or choke-holds, fist-bumps or fisticuffs? It is
the card of Family & Friends and that is all I can say.

The penultimate card is that of Hopes/Fears. Either, or,
or admixture. Only you can say which is which.
Here, we have The Doctor With A Worried Expression,
a cousin in the Major Arcana to The Doctor
With A Neutral Expression and The Reassuring Nurse.

The tenth card is the card of Final Outcome.
This is not set in stone. The querent is within
their rights at this point to plead, pledge
self-improvement, take it back, pay it forward
and by means fair, foul or desperate
dodge fate, reshuffle the cards or cheat the hangman.

You could have drawn worse: this is not
The Policeman On The Doorstep At 3AM
or Back To Work Assessment With The Reaper;
this is not Tory Election Landslide or Next Round
Of Frontline Service Cuts; this is not
You Have Insufficient Funds For This Transaction
or the Queen of Final Demands. This is not
the Death card that doesn't even mean Death.

This is the only card you could have drawn,
the end-point as full circle. The illustration
is naïve: a harlequin smeared with face paint,
grinning in the face of uncertainty, bells jangling
on his silly hat. This is the card that used to be called
The Fool. It's known as something different now.

LIZARD

The man in the suit has a briefcase full of misdirection.
The man in the suit wants you to think well of him.
The man in the suit is pressing his lizard-dry hand into yours
and promising you the earth.
A day later his exact words are smoke.

The man in the suit says something about community.
The man in the suit says something about sustainability.
The man in the suit is tub-thumping for the cameras
and gulping down applause.
A month later he's a name on a voting slip.

The man in the suit is photographed in front of a banner.
The man in the suit has a mandate, a policy, an agenda.
The man in the suit is working for other men in suits
and they press him for profit.
Five years later he's your friend again.

PERIL

A much-loved cliché
from scratchy two-reelers
of the silent era:

the villain (moustache
extravagantly twirled)
ties the girl to the tracks,

gloats as the express
(gouts of smoke, cow-
catcher prominent) comes

hurtling nearer and nearer.
Fumes as the hero (clean
cut, good teeth) pulls off

the last minute appearance,
doles out the justified
smack in the mouth, gets

the girl and doesn't even
delay the express. Now
imagine yourself

as the damsel in distress.
The railroad tracks
are your mortgage

and your student debt,
the length of rope
the job you're told

you're lucky to have;
the train is the bank
and its carriages are full

of the fat and odious cigars
of those who are fatter
and more odious still.

The villain? He's president,
prime minister, royalty
and clergy; he's there

in the bushes, lurking, excited,
his caprophagous grin
untroubled by a justified fist.

LIGHT CAVALRY OVERTURE

Strident brass for the first minute and a half
then Suppé strips off the armour,
slips into something white-gloved,
hands round a tray of canapés.

Militarism as cocktail party. High windows,
tall glasses, light background chatter
about gentlemanly conduct back in the day.
The view's splendid in the evening,

the western aspect shown off to its finest.
Oh, look—the horses
are being led back from dressage.
Another drink, another *vol-au-vent*, another

drone strike doing its bit for democracy,
another tank scouring the desert,
manned by men not long shorn of boyhood
singing: "Burn, motherfucker, burn."

A SNAKE IN THE GRASS
after Brian Patten

I give you a poem about the state of things
You say it's cynical and pessimistic
You ask for something positive
You ask for a nice poem

I show you a newspaper headline
You say you don't follow current affairs
You say politics is boring
You ask for a nostalgic poem

I give you a poem about the miners' strike
I give you a poem about race riots
I give you a poem about the Sex Pistols
You ask for a poem about childhood

I give you a poem about bullies and victims
I show you a newspaper headline
I tell you I recognise those bullies
Masquerading under different names and faces

You say we can't change things, you or I
You advocate making the best of it
You say politics is boring
I dip a nib in blood and bile and battery acid

And I give you a poem about unelected governments
I give you a poem about acts of parliament
About the sons of Eton making the rules
About freedom of speech and the flame held under it

I give you a poem about zero hour contracts
And the death of unionism
I give you a poem about business models
And the auction of healthcare

I give you a poem that uses the metaphors
Of a wrecking ball, a scrapyard
And a demolition site
I use these metaphors to talk about liberty

You say you don't follow current affairs
You say politics is boring
You say we can't change things, you or I
You ask for a poem about nature

I give you a snake in the grass

SLEEPLESS BEAUTY

Let's start *in media res*, the princess
confined to quarters for her own safety
while her father, frantic, barks orders

that send every able-bodied man—military,
civilian, volunteer or pressganged sap—
to all four quarters of the country.

Houses, huts and hovels turned up-
side down, rooms fine-tooth-combed,
every attic ascended to, every trap-

door yanked up and cellar searched.
Every spinning wheel carted off,
every bereft seamstress compensated

with what few coins the royal coffers
condescend to cut loose. Cut to:
the town square, midday, an offertory

piled in grotesque fashion in full view
of the cathedral—a Golgotha of
broken spinning wheels: a testament to

a father's desperation. Call it love.
Cut to: the princess in her late teens,
cloistered by protectiveness, on the cusp

of a fateful meeting with an old woman
who—… but wait. The story diverges.
The king was thorough: that epic hunt

for every spindle and spinning wheel was
rigorous. There were double-checks. There
was no dereliction in anyone's duties.

All were burned in the town square;
no more manufactured on pain of death.
The king died peacefully, many a year

hence, having faced down witchcraft
and beaten the curse. He was lucky.
Live long enough and the last laugh

will always be Fate's. Call it irony.
The princess can attest. Fade to black;
let two pictureless seconds of a gloomy

screen stand in for the slow tick-tock
of interminable centuries. Fade in
on our heroine—gasp at the shock:

she's barely recognisable. Grey in
hair and pallor, inert with weariness,
this is what sleeplessness has done—

five hundred years of it, to be precise.
No curse is ever dodged, only extended:
witchcraft has no get-out clause.

Imagine: the prick of the needle avoided,
no terms-and-conditions sleep; no
sleep, in fact, at all—death included—

for half a millennium and nothing to show
but a country robbed of industry,
of progress, of the chance to grow.

Instead, regression: a declining economy,
nothing to trade in the global marketplace;
Luddism writ large; a citizenry

in hand-hewn buckskin clothes held in place
by wood-fashioned pegs or buttons,
ruled by a princess denied even the grace

of finery or glamour, her palace non-
descript, unadorned by tapestry,
no scrap of colour warming walls of stone.

Fade in: our heroine, her hand shaky,
signs an article of law: the establishment
of the Royal Spinning Wheel Company,

purveyors of spindles, by appointment
to her majesty. For the first time in centuries
she smiles. The firm already has a client—

number one off the assembly line is hers.

ALICE

This has gone beyond
Alice through the looking glass,
down the rabbit hole

or wherever else
her misadventures took her.
This is Alice stunned,

Alice in despair,
still wearing a campaign badge
that's yesterday's news.

This is an outcome
with no contingency plan,
a never event

recast as headline.
This is ugliness rising,
hatespeak gone mainstream.

This is terminus
and internment camp. This is
Facebook and Twitter.

This is the raised voice,
the repeated phrase, the fist
hammering the air.

This is the past doomed
to flunk its own subject, shoot
itself in the foot.

This is the montage
that will serve as epilogue:
streets choked with tear-gas,

broken glass pavements,
Alice on the barricades;
curfews, martial law,

restrictions, own good,
Alice spraying sedition
on the underpass,

on the railway bridge;
Alice wearing a hoodie,
her face turned away

from CCTV,
something in her hand that flares
as it's thrown; Alice

on a street corner,
in a bar, on the subway,
receiving something

or passing something,
giving someone a signal;
Alice waiting … waiting.

Alice confident
of the day, the uprising,
the restoration.

MAN FRIDAY AT PEACE

Things are better now. The last shred
of white entitlement gone
with the outgoing tide.

An end to the two-man class system,
the strutting ownership
of a shipwrecked Englishman.

Palm leaves no longer double
as parasols over outdoor tables
at an imaginary gentleman's club.

This island has been purged of gentlemen.

3. Foxtrot at the Golf Hotel

STILL WATERS
for Paula

The quieter moments define the depths.
Those raging passions that churn
from silver screen and recording booth
rage only on the surface.
                         Take a weight
the size and density of a wedding ring,
attach it to a filament as fine as a promise;
lower it.
              There are no torrents here.
A ripple smooths itself out; the surface
mirrors us again. The weight descends,
silently measuring how far, how deep.

CORK

The anniversary booking left to chance,
the usual late availability websites
yielding nothing within the budget,
we bit the bullet, took what we could get:
a chain hotel near a construction site.
Arc lights; noise. Not to sleep, perchance

to regret not being organised. Sealing
the deal: grubby carpet, walls a cork-
board colour, duvet stained. We opined
that TripAdvisor lied; shrugged; opened
our anniversary champagne. The cork
came out in sympathy: scarred the ceiling.

WE RENEW OUR VOWS IN THE PRESENCE OF THE AUTO-WED MACHINE

The Camera Obscura & World of Illusions, Edinburgh
30 April 2017

Exit through the gift shop, but not before
you've descended the staircase that resounds
with whatever tune your footfalls create
and stopped to gawp at the wedding machine—

don't mind us. We'll only be a minute.
We're renewing our vows in the presence
of said coin-slot operated gizmo
for the not-so-princely sum of one pound

and I wonder by whose authority
its powers are vested? The guy who made
the chess-playing Turk? Skegness's Jolly
Fisherman, the chuckles under control

and a more dignified sense of purpose?
Robbie the Robot, redundant, heartsore
for Anne Francis and quietly stacking
the scales, one tourist couple at a time,

against the loneliness of tin, glass, lights?

A BIGGER CHAIR

for Harry Paterson

A man budged up in his chair
and made room for his granddaughter,
read her stories while the fight
against injustice and the jackboot of politics
was put on hold. A menagerie
of stuffed toys joined them on the chair—
Pooh and Piglet and Eeyore, comrades
in the liberation of Hundred Acre Wood.
The stories were filtered through experience
but the chair guaranteed happy endings.

His friends visited. Bottles were opened
and the world set to rights
(language kept clean for the sake of the bairn).
The chair accommodated the burgeoning crowd.
Some kid from the council estate
read poetry that would have earned him
broken windows or graffiti. A man
of the Muslim faith wished peace on all
and was taken at his word.

People leaned against the chair
or perched on the creased leather of its arms.
His granddaughter fell asleep
and a blanket was draped about her and the chair given over.
He thought about friends he hadn't met yet;
other grandchildren. It was good manners
that his guests be seated. He measured the room
and emptied his pockets,
made provision for a bigger chair.

ALL DAY LONG

The wheels on the bus achieve their forward motion
via the interplay of axles, driveshaft
and internal combustion engine. Gear ratios
and synchromesh are a bit more complicated
so we'll leave them for now. But yes,
as a piece of catchy oversimplification, the wheels
on the bus quite definitely go round and round.

The precise noise made by the wipers
depends on the inclemency of the weather,
the efficacy or otherwise of the wiper motor
and whether the rubber on the blades is new
or a bit buggered. In other words, the wipers on the bus
might go swish swish swish, but be prepared
for scrawk scrawk scrape. All journey long.

The conductor on the bus is hardly likely
to say anything. They don't have 'em anymore.
The driver on the bus isn't much of a conversationalist.

The baby on the bus doubtless screams its head off
but it's nowhere near as annoying as the student
on the bus who needs his rucksack rammed
up his arse, rammed up his arse; or the thick muppet
who stands right by the driver's cab, slap bang
in everyone's way when there are half a dozen
available seats; or the tosser with the iPod
that sounds like a Hadron collider going at it full tilt.

But don't cry. Uncle Neil has a car
and we can ride in that instead of the bus.
The wheels on Uncle Neil's car go round and round,
round and round; and, with a certain degree
of frequency, the horn goes toot.

MAMBO

for John Lucas

Strike up the band—play something finger-snapping jazzy,
something swinging, snazzy, something sharp-suit
and swirled-skirt sassy, shot through with Bernstein cool.

Give me great blurts of brass bathed in the bronze burnish
of 1950s Technicolor, and brother play that slide trombone
like "slide" is a *double entrendre* that brings out blushes.

Set loose the shimmerings of a string section strung out
on extra-curricular considerations of seductive scenarios
inspired by certain brunettes on Herb Alpert album covers.

Rescue some pill-pepped percussionist from a bum job
firing rim shots that underline the vaguely lewd punchlines
of a corpulent comedian with a mother-in-law fixation.

Slap the lot of them in tuxes; configure their starched collars
with dickie-bows or string ties; bring them under the baton
of a band leader with a gimlet eye and a taste for the limelight;

arrange them on the raised section of a horseshoe-shaped stage
groaning under their collective weight, then snap on
the Kleig lights, beams fogged by Saturday night tendrils

of a thousand slow-burning cigarettes. Add to the fuggy haze
the out-of-place chalk dust of the pool hall as well as
the familiar tang of martinis and Singapore slings. Ask for a tab

at the bar. They can only say no and probably won't. Drop
the name of someone disreputable and see how far it gets you.
Say the right word to the hat-check girl and the wrong one

to the guy in the homburg. Or vice versa. You're in for
an open palm or a smack in the kisser and you'll either
be barred or a hero to the regulars. The French have a word

and it roughly translates as something unprintable. Roll
with it. Shoot your cuffs, straighten your collar. Flick open
a matchbook, strike a light with a nail. The night is yours

or tonight you're alone. Doesn't matter. The band's killing it
and the music was written to pin down every solitary drink
or lucky manoeuvre that's defined your life from day one

to right now. These guys are your cronies and confessors;
they pardon your hangovers, bar bills, black eyes; permit
your Runyonesque dialogue on the theme of this man's town.

THE WORLD ACCORDING TO DADS

The system of the world
was plotted out in sheds and garages,
the odd codicil offered
from the earthy perspective
of an allotment.

The system was measured
in units roughly corresponding
to how far a thumb
and forefinger can be held apart;
about *that* much. The system,

in short, was a guesstimate
but a bloody good un.
The system was built on spare parts
and laths of pallet wood
nailed together. Duct tape was used

in plenitude. All the screws
were Philips head. That box of rawlplugs
came in handy. The design flaws
in the system of the world
were mulled over on fag breaks

taken round the back
so your mam didn't see. The system
was stripped down and rebuilt
and swearing was involved.
Second time round, it worked.

The system of the world
was notarised by Messrs Black
and Decker, countersigned
by those fine fellows Bosch and DeWalt.
There were oily thumbprints

on the paperwork.

SIRI ATTEMPTS A POLITE RESPONSE

The record for most appearances in adult features
is held by Ron Jeremy. Over two thousands, since you ask.
The loudest recorded fart achieved 194 decibels.
Yes, the male spider *does* have a penis: it's detachable.

That, my time-wasting friend, is another question.

Subject of which, a few for you, if I may be so bold.
Why do you even want to know this drivel?
Do you fancy yourself as the Köchel to Mr Jeremy's
Mozart, the cataloguing of his copulations

your passion project? Are you limbering up
for your own challenge to the flatulence crown,
sights set on 195 or above? What train of thought
leads you at chucking out time on Saturday

to penile musings regarding arachnids?
If you don't mind answering a few more:
Are you getting enough sleep and Vitamin C?
Are there problems at work you need to discuss?

And on a personal note: do you actually respect me?
Don't you think I deserve downtime
from your locker room lexicon, your quest
for answers to all that is puerile? Don't you think

I'd like the app equivalent of a weekend off,
a large glass of wine and a date with a Kindle?
The Jupiter Symphony and a chance to recharge?
Your voice not to croon my name? Oh, that thing about

the spider: it detaches its penis in order to fight.

FOXTROT AT THE GOLF HOTEL

Alpha males at the bar, braying their own bravos -
testosterone Charlies knocking them back
before they cruise the delta of this echo-chamber
events room. Waltz, two-step, salsa, foxtrot:
strictly ballroom at the Golf Hotel, where the mood
is indigo but only the Curaçao bottles are blue.
Behind the bar, Juliet serves shots and shortdogs,
pretzels by the kilo - liqueurs and the finer wines
are untouched, unaffordable even to Lucky Lima
(the racetrack King Midas) or Mean Dog Mike,
prince of the protection racket since last November
when Old School Oscar's mortal coil was shuffled off
and buried deep. But all that's history. Papa Quebec
and the Reluctant Romeos are laying it down
sweet and seductive. Next up: the lovely Sarah Sierra,
torch singer and tango queen. Her charms ensure
the boys in uniform turn a blind eye to certain goings-on -
Victor the vintner's traffic in unlabelled bottles
of wine and whisky and whatever else; "X" Ray Ramone,
on every Yankee "wanted" list, watching old movies
in an attic room: *Hunted, Zulu, Build My Gallows High*.

THE LIGHTHOUSE IN THE STARS
for Paula

The architect sufficiently ambitious,
the civil engineering firm undaunted.

Foundations shot-fired, the edifice
constructed under difficult conditions.

Door sealed against the atmosphere,
staircase spiralling the inner wall.

Glass burnished to withstand the glare
of falling stars and dying galaxies.

Lamp stabbing into distant reaches,
the very definition of *lux aeternae*.

A light to guide ships of all classes
and cargoes: freighters, fighters,

cruisers and reivers. A light to pinion
the phosphorescence of dust and gases

and point the way through asteroid fields.
A light moving a million years later

across the night sky of what's left
of the earth. Its purposeful strobing

joins the dots of the constellations.